SRA
Reasoning
and Writing

Workbook 1

Level B

Siegfried Engelmann
Ann Brown Arbogast
Karen Lou Seitz Davis

McGraw Hill Education

Cover Credits: (t)© Ingram Publishing/Alamy,
(b)Alan Sealls/WeatherVideoHD.TV

mheducation.com/prek-12

Send all inquiries to:
McGraw-Hill Education
8787 Orion Place
Columbus, OH 43240

ISBN: 978-0-02-684759-9
MHID: 0-02-684759-0

Printed in the United States of America.

26 27 28 LKV 22 21

Lesson 1

A.

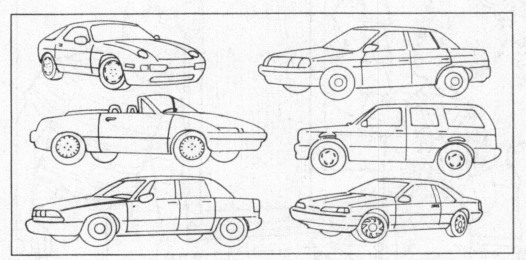

B.

1. true   false
2. true   false
3. true   false
4. true   false

C.

Lesson 2

A.

B.

1. true false
2. true false
3. true false
4. true false

C.

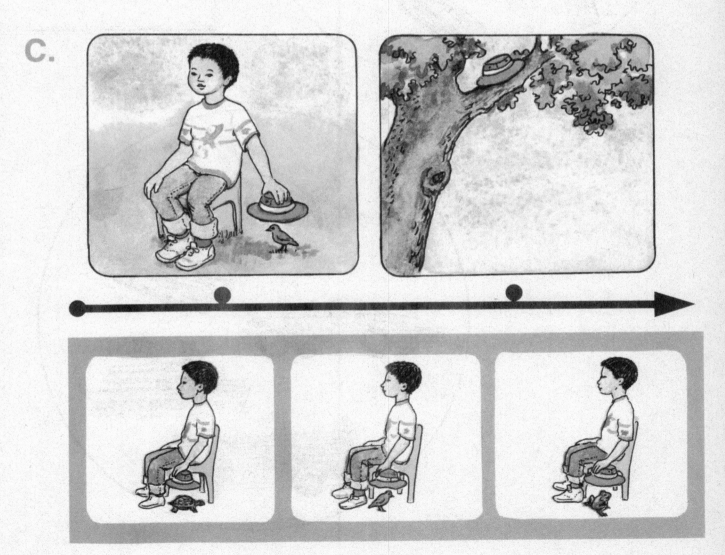

D.

1.

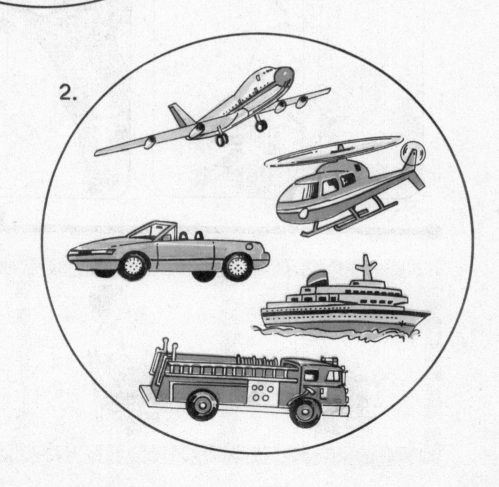

2.

E.

1. true   false

2. true   false

3. true   false

4. true   false

5. true   false

6. true   false

7. true   false

F.

Lesson 3

A.

1. _____

2. _____

3. _____

4. _____

5. _____

B.

C.

1. true   false

2. true   false

3. true   false

4. true   false

D.

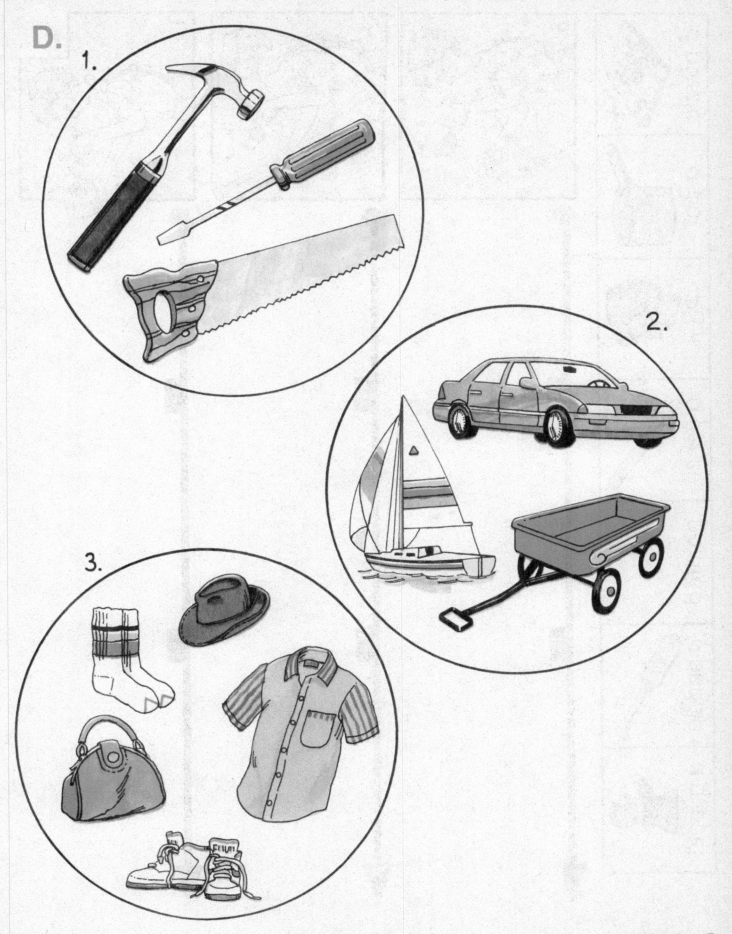

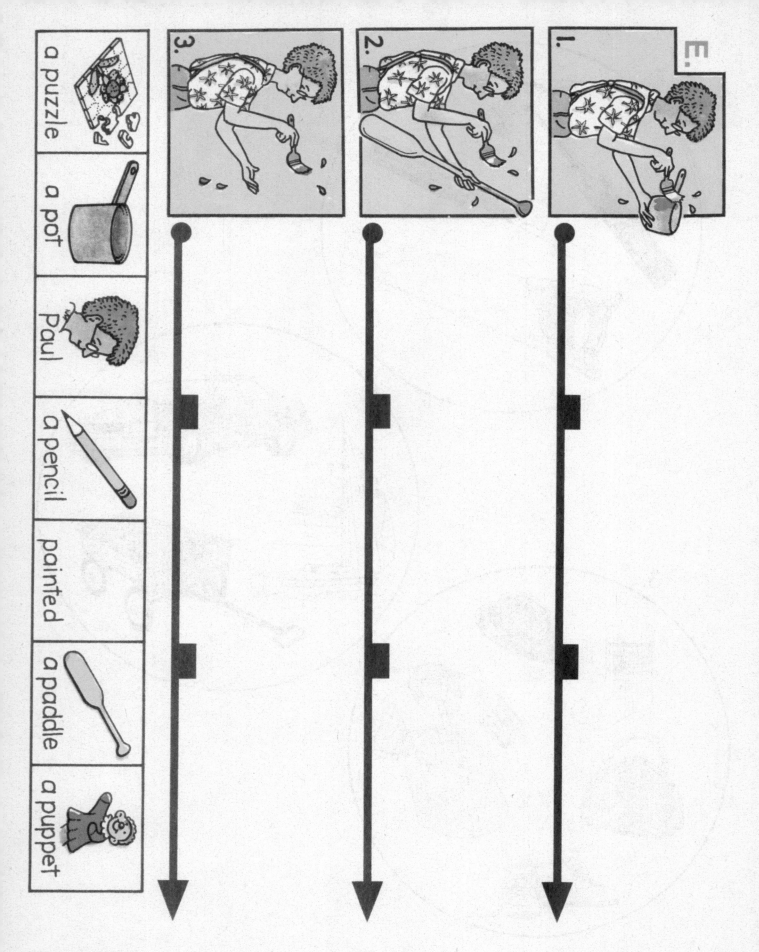

F.

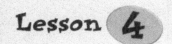

A.

B.

1. true   false

2. true   false

3. true   false

4. true   false

5. true   false

C.

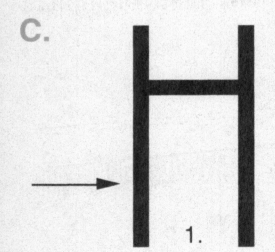

1.

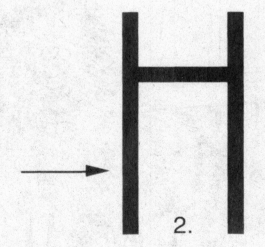

2.

D.

Lesson 5

A.   Some of the bugs have spots.

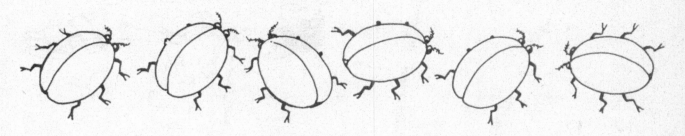

B.   1. true   false   2. true   false

3. true   false   4. true   false

C.

| hammer | bus | socks | truck | saw |

| hat | shirt | drill | car |

| 1. Tools | 2. Clothing | 3. Vehicles |

_____ _____ _____

_____ _____ _____

_____ _____ _____

Lesson 6

A.   None of the apples have a stem.

B.

1. Before you changed the picture, _____ of the apples had a stem.

2. After you changed the picture, _____ of the apples had a stem.

C.

1.

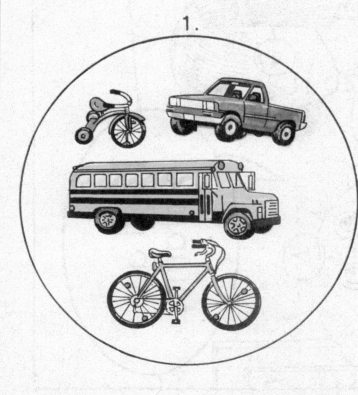

2.

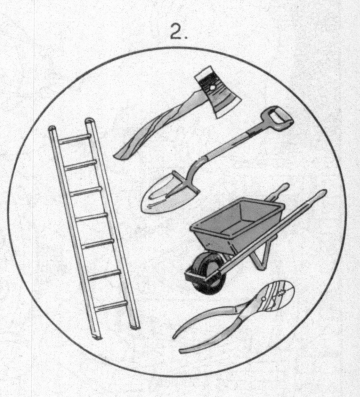

D.

E.

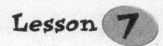

Lesson 7

A.

B.

1. true   false
2. true   false
3. true   false

1. Some of the flowers have leaves. _____

2. None of the flowers have leaves. _____

C.

carrot   owl   church   banana   turtle

bear   house   hamburger   barn

1. Food	2. Buildings	3. Animals

_____ _____ _____

_____ _____ _____

_____ _____ _____

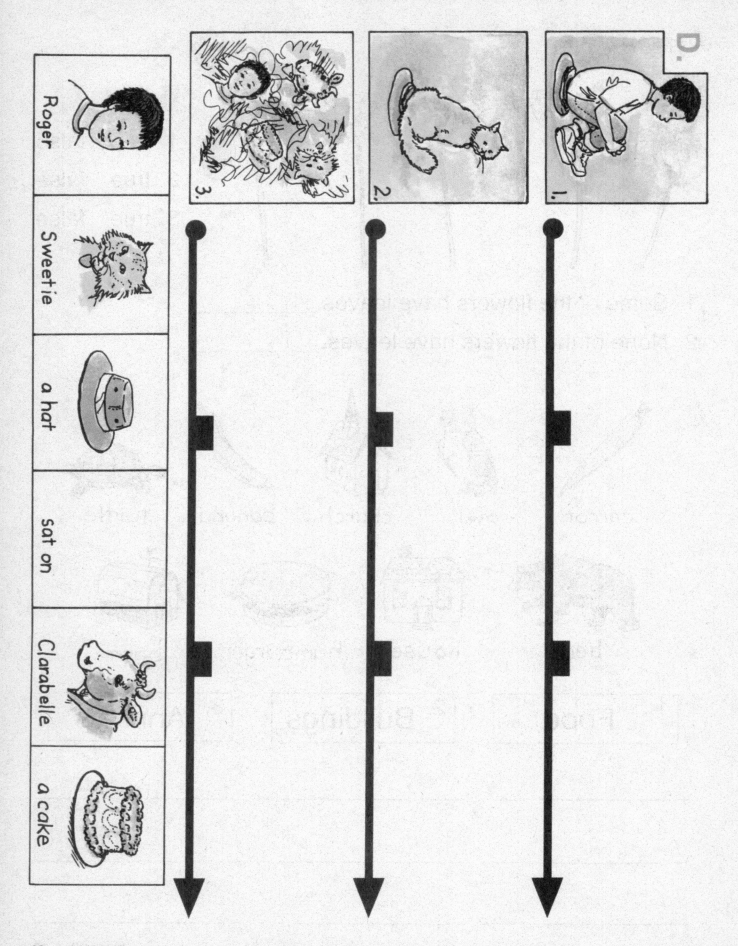

E.

1. bud   2. yus   3. fud   4. ugg

_____   _____   _____

A.

B.

1. egg shells
2. Ben met 5 men.
3. I had ten pets.

C.

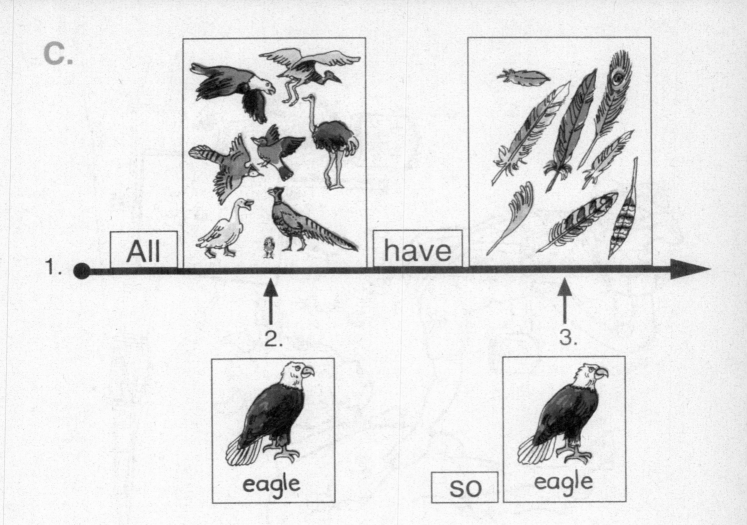

1.

2.

3.

Lesson 9

A.

1. ●━━━━━━━━━━●━━━━━━━━➤

2.   ●━━━━━━━━━━━●━━━➤

B.

□   □

a fan   a hat   a ball   a goat   a sheep   Clarabelle

1. The third object to Bleep's right is _____.

2. The first object to Bleep's left is _____.

3. The first object to Bleep's right is _____.

4. The second object to Bleep's _____ is _____.

C.

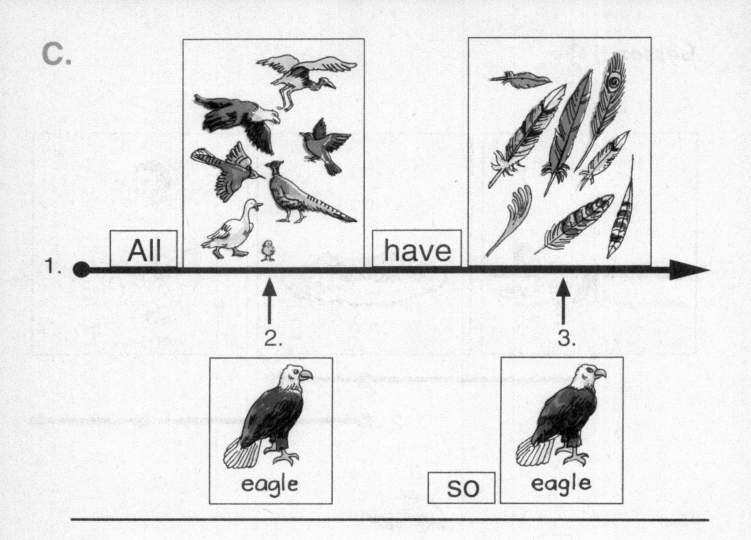

1. **All** ... **have** →

2. ↑ **eagle**

3. ↑ **SO** **eagle**

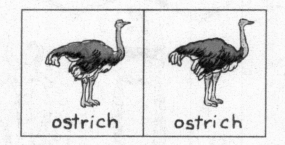

ostrich | ostrich

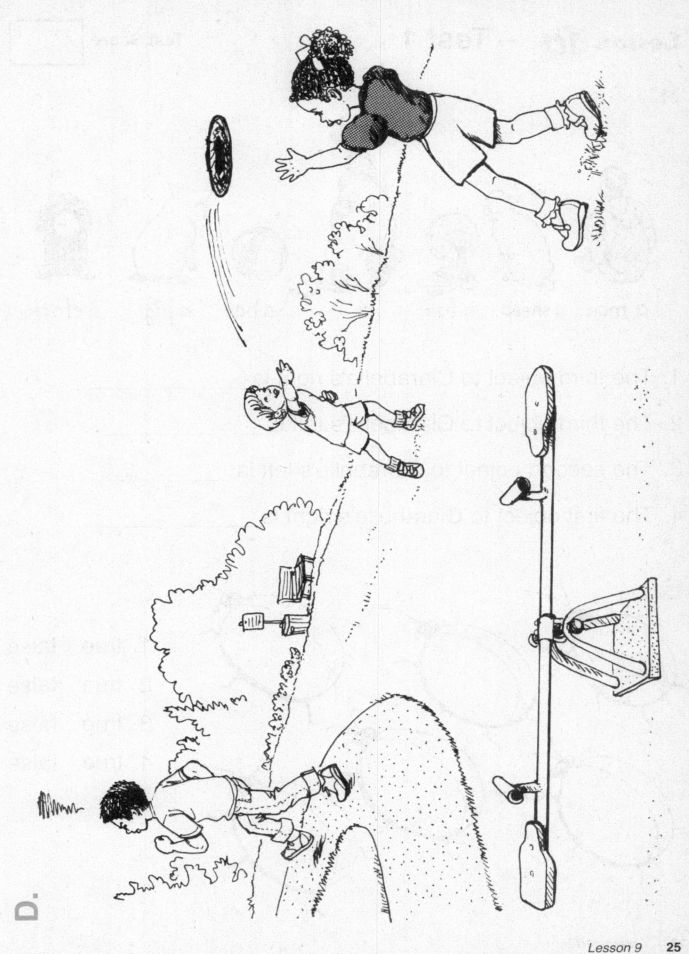

D.

Test Score [ ]

A.

a man   a sheep   a fan   a ball   a pig   a clock

1. The third object to Clarabelle's right is _____.

2. The third object to Clarabelle's left is _____.

3. The second object to Clarabelle's left is _____.

4. The first object to Clarabelle's right is _____.

B.

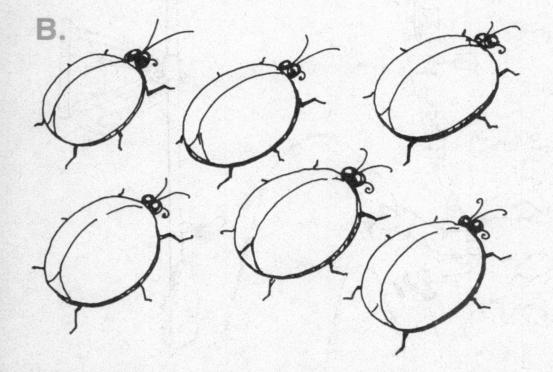

C.

1. true   false

2. true   false

3. true   false

4. true   false

Lesson 11

A.

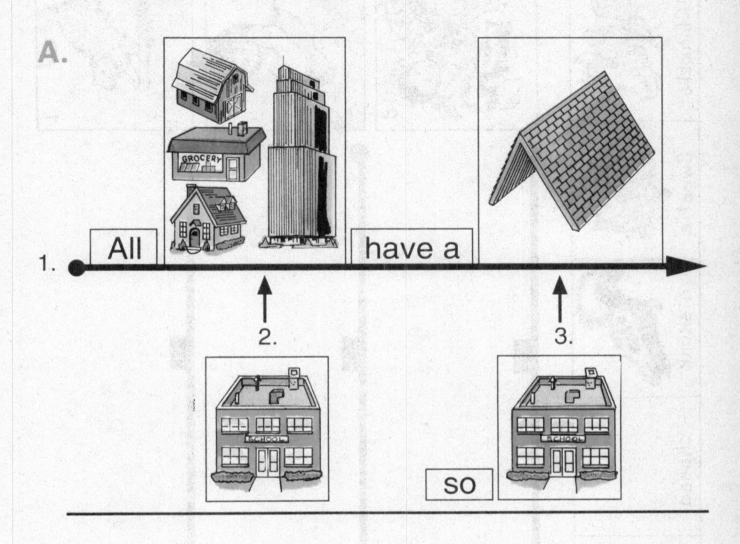

1. All [buildings] have a [roof] so [school] so [school]

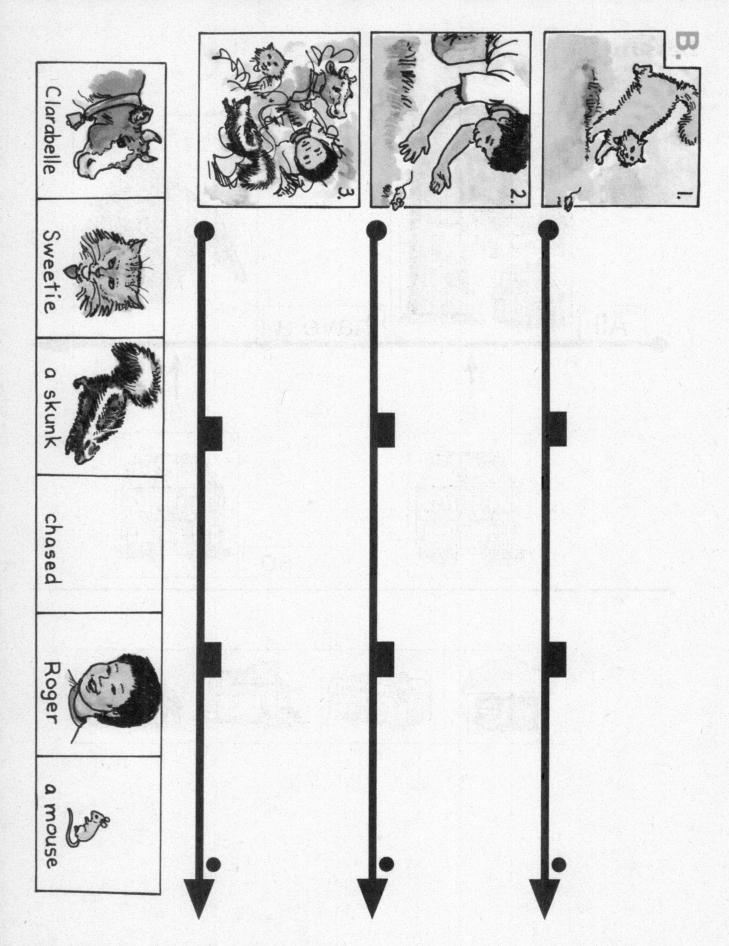

C.

A.

B.

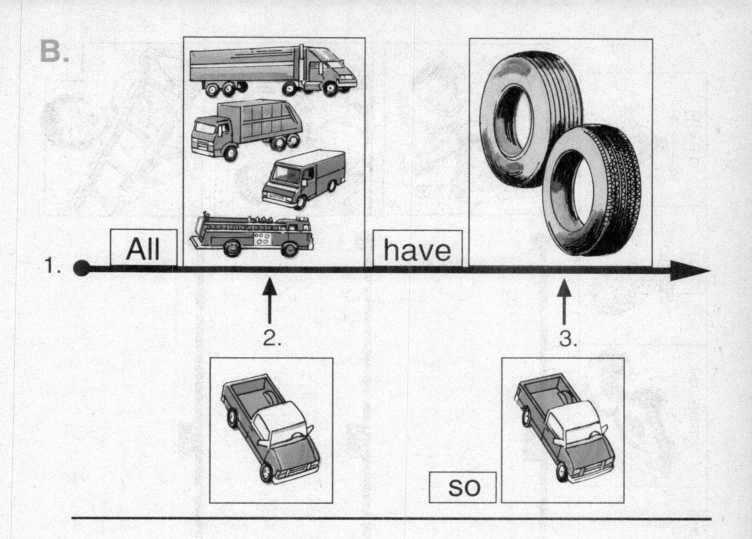

1. [All] ... [have]

2.

3.

[so]

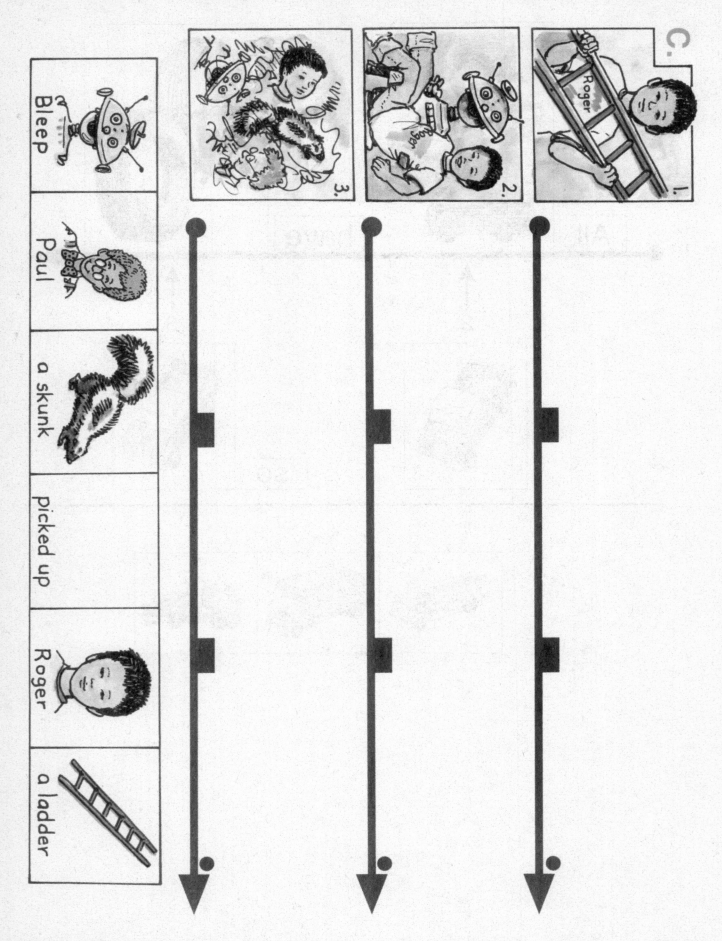

D.

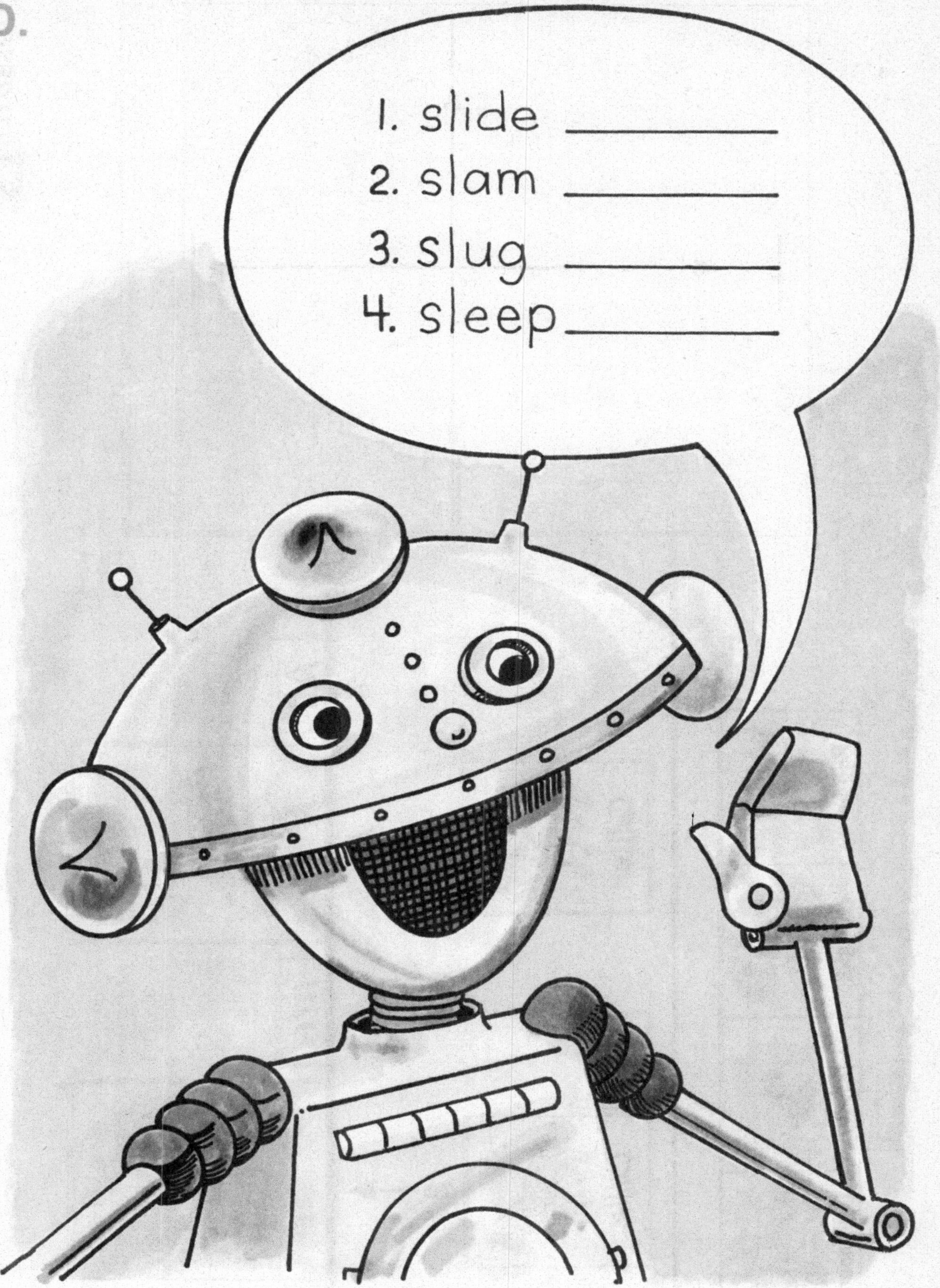

1. slide _____
2. slam _____
3. slug _____
4. sleep _____

A.

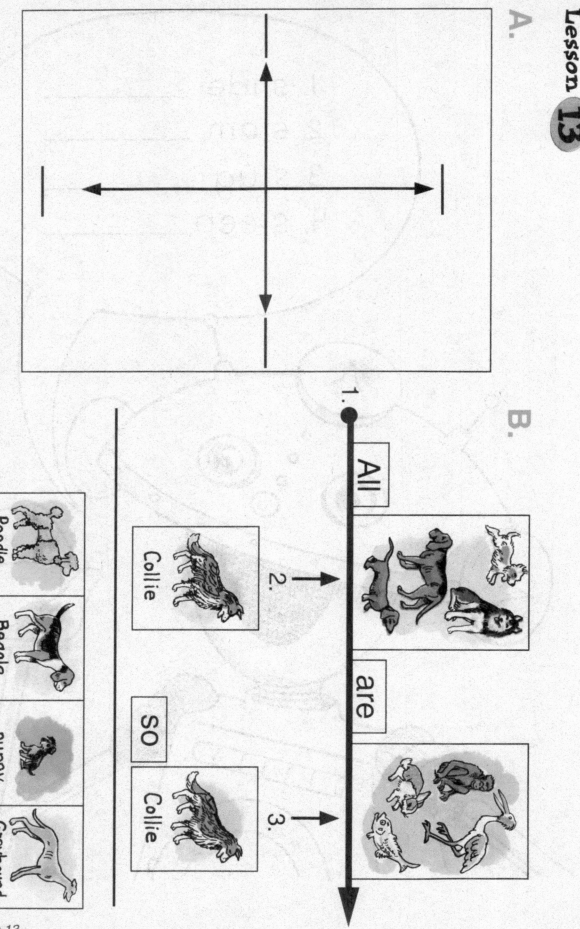

B.

1. All are

2. Collie

3. so Collie

Poodle Beagle puppy Greyhound

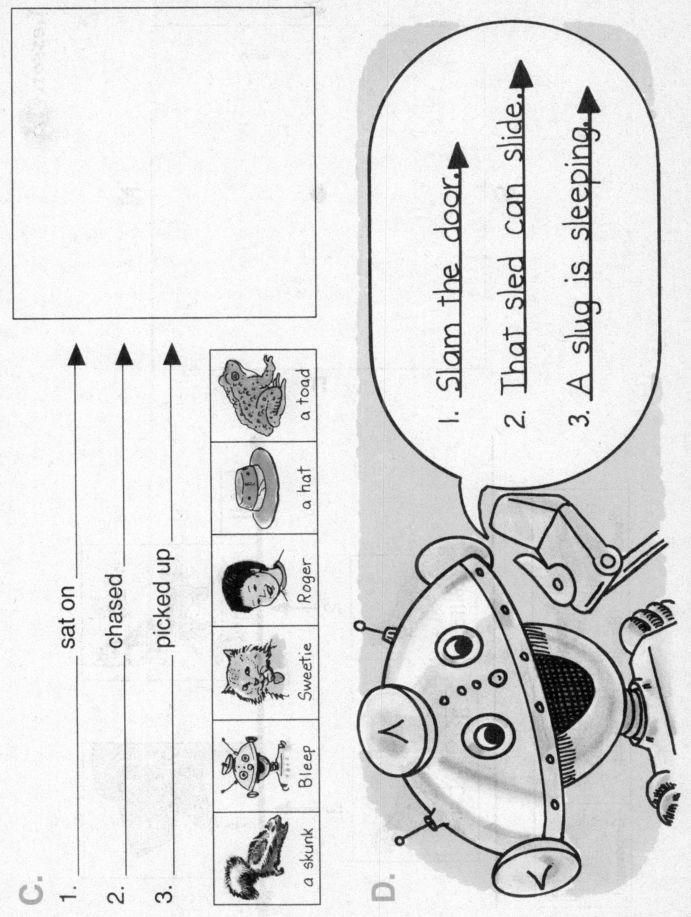

C.

1. _____ sat on _____

2. _____ chased _____

3. _____ picked up _____

| a skunk | Bleep | Sweetie | Roger | a hat | a toad |

D.

1. Slam the door.

2. That sled can slide.

3. A slug is sleeping.

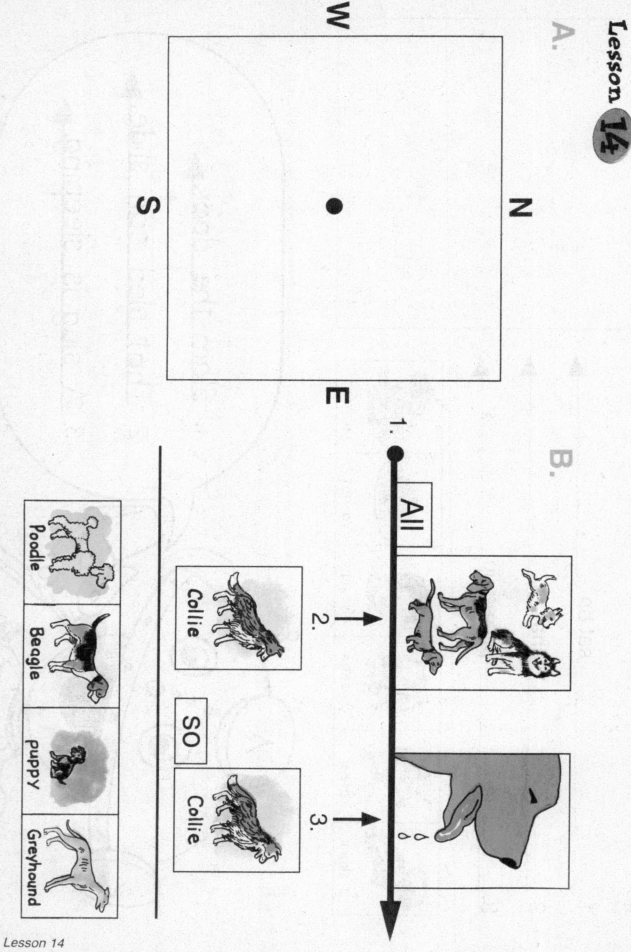

C.

D.

A.

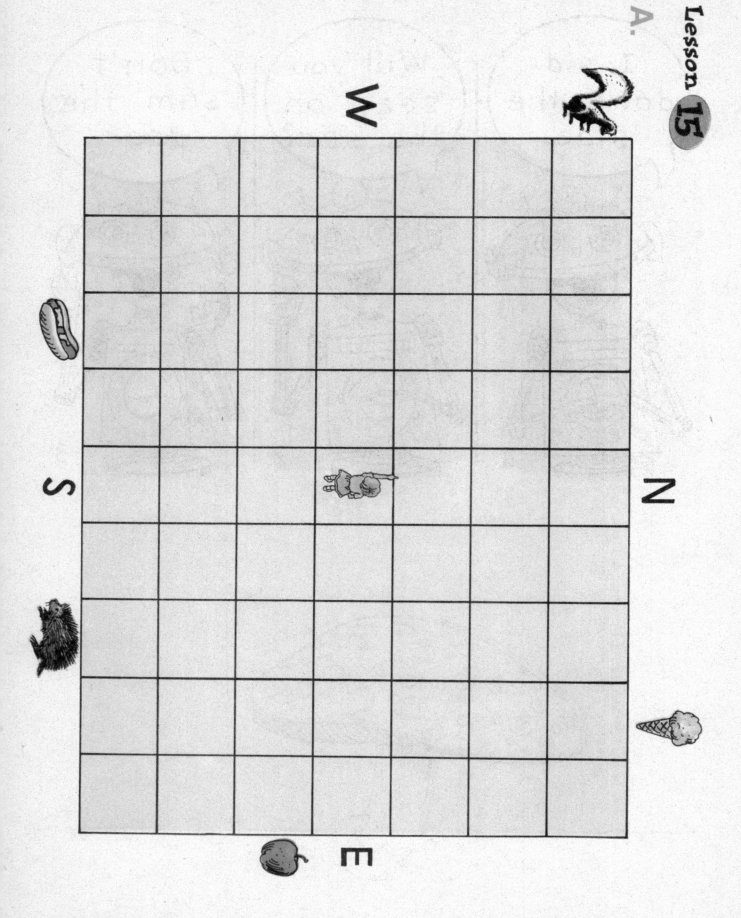

B.

1. All ... are

2. fire truck

SO fire truck

3.

C.

1. _____ hugged _____ ➤

2. _____ washed _____ ➤

3. _____ talked to _____ ➤

| a skunk | Sweetie | a hat | Roger | a clown | Bleep |

D.

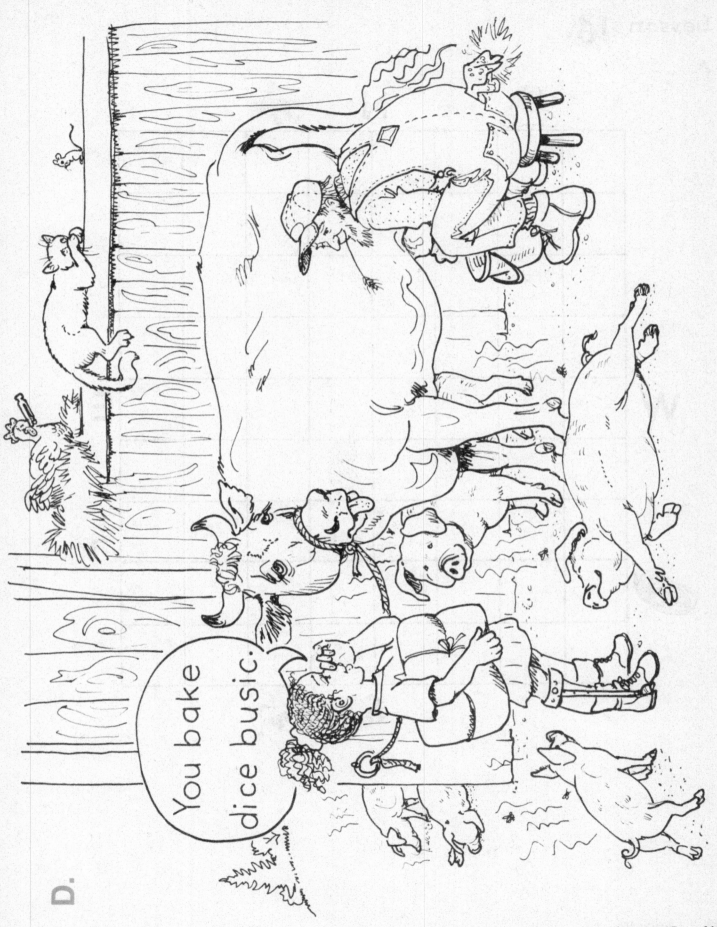

Lesson 16

A.

B.

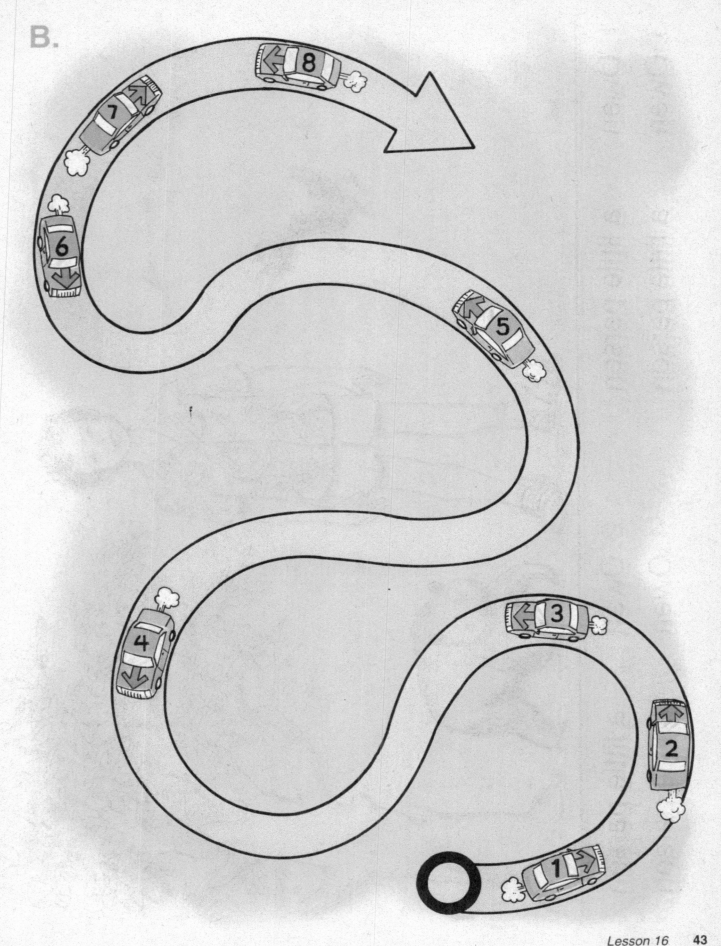

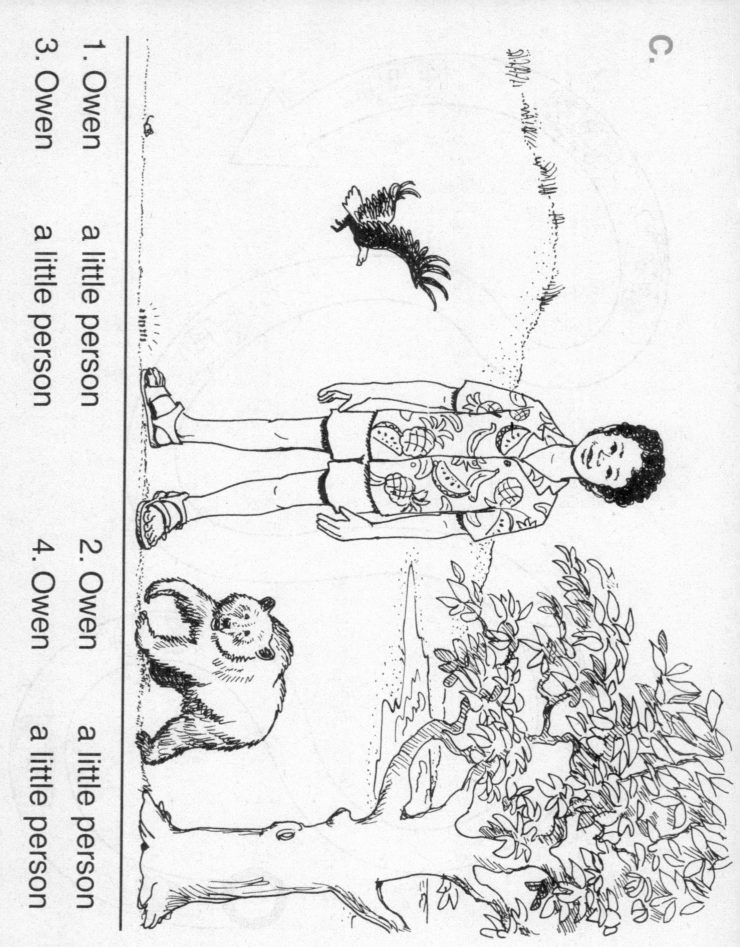

C.

1. Owen   a little person

2. Owen   a little person

3. Owen   a little person

4. Owen   a little person

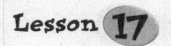

A.

1. _____ smelled _____ ➤

2. _____ held _____ ➤

3. _____ kissed _____ ➤

the soap | Goober | a skunk | Molly

Owen | a hat | Bleep | Clarabelle

B.

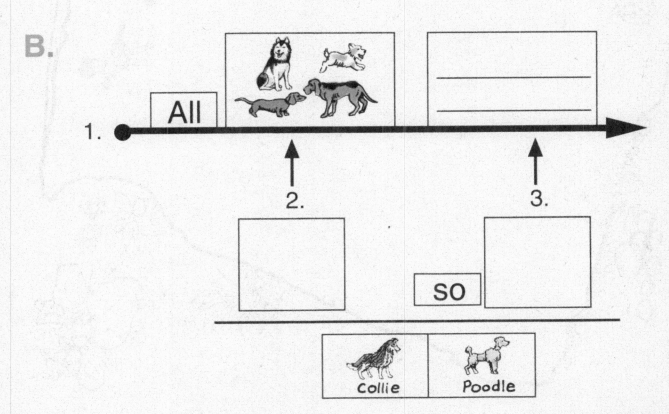

1. ● All _____ _____ ➤

2.

3.

SO

Collie | Poodle

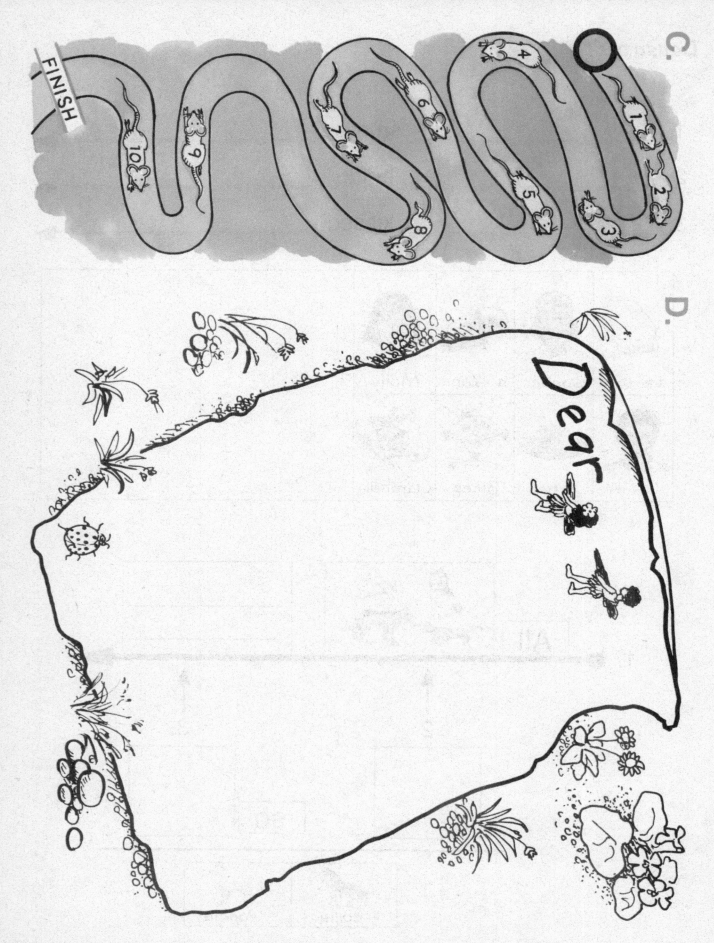

FINISH

Dear

E.

Dear Owen,

~~Our names are Fizz and Liz~~

~~Hello, my name is Owen~~

we
and ~~I~~ live on a beautiful island.

This island is very small.

There are many small animals

on this island.

We have tiny bears and tigers

and alligators.

We have tiny rabbits.

We also have lots of tiny birds.

The biggest of the tiny birds

is the eagle.

We have bugs that are so small

you can hardly see them.

A.

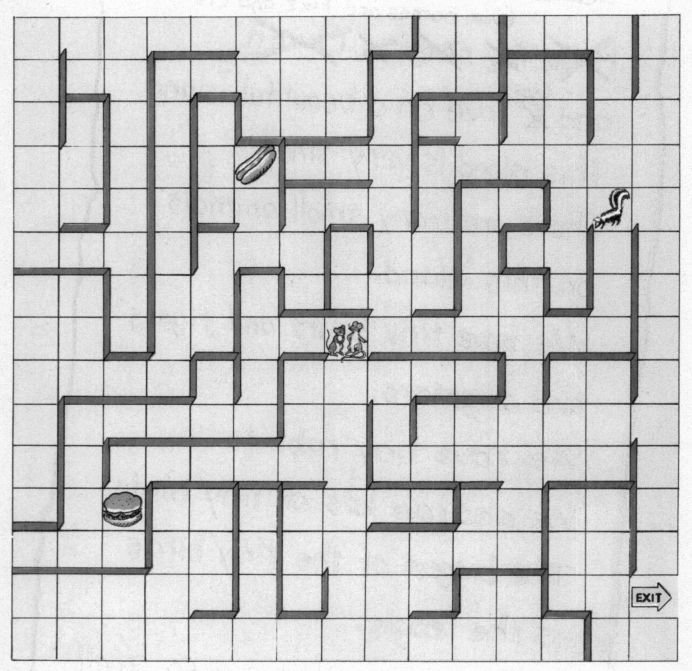

B.

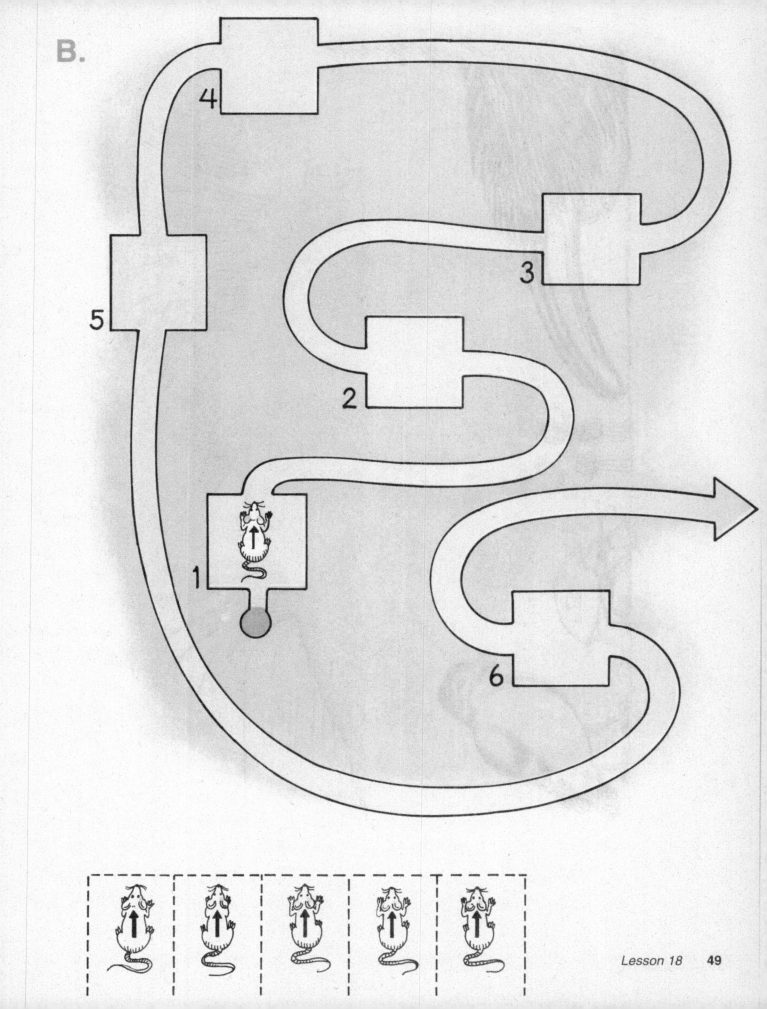

Lesson 19

A.

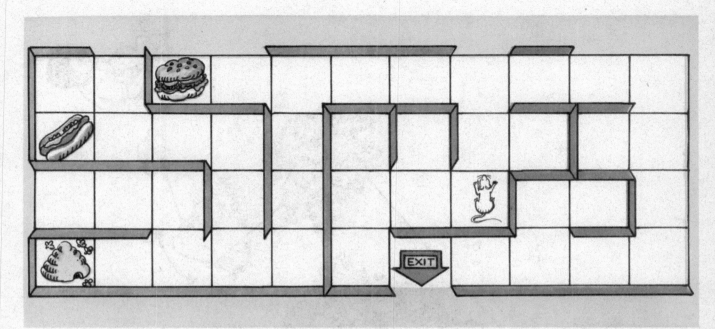

Bragging Rat

Bragging Rat

1. Two squares to the north.
2. Three squares to the east.
3. Three squares to the south.
4. Four squares to the west.

1. Two squares to the north.
2. Three squares to the west.
3. Three squares to the south.
4. Four squares to the west.

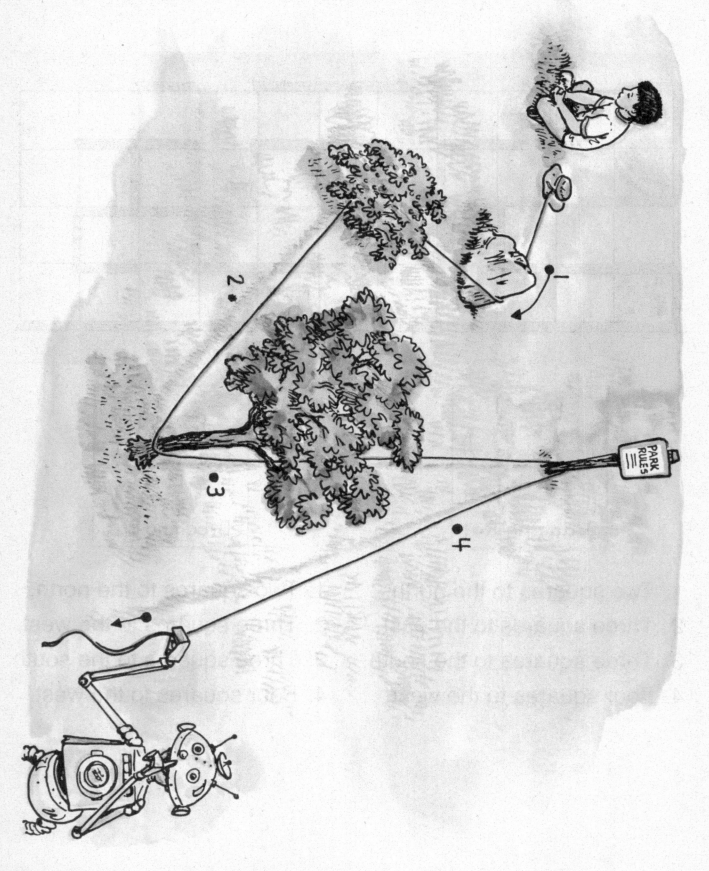

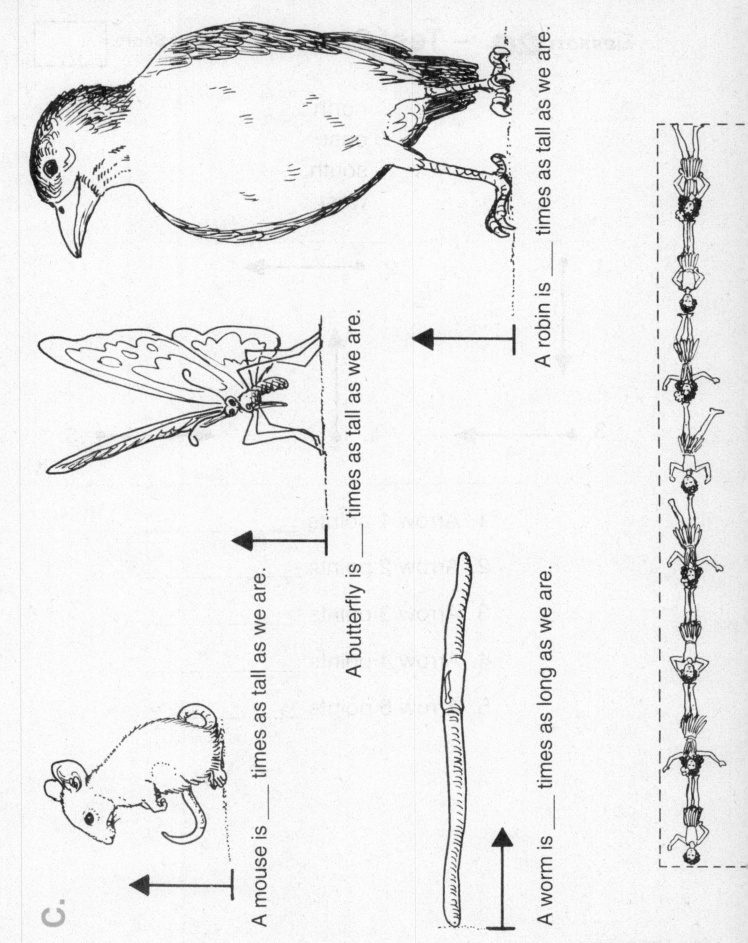

A robin is ___ times as tall as we are.

A butterfly is ___ times as tall as we are.

A mouse is ___ times as tall as we are.

A worm is ___ times as long as we are.

C.

A.

north
east
south
west

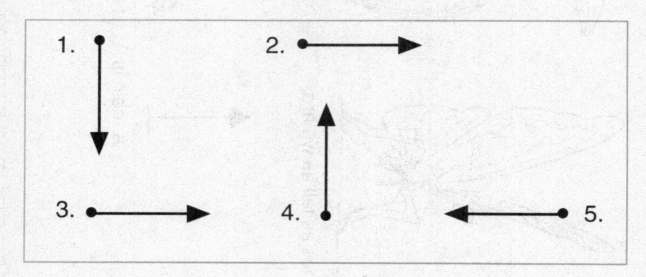

1. Arrow 1 points _____.

2. Arrow 2 points _____.

3. Arrow 3 points _____.

4. Arrow 4 points _____.

5. Arrow 5 points _____.

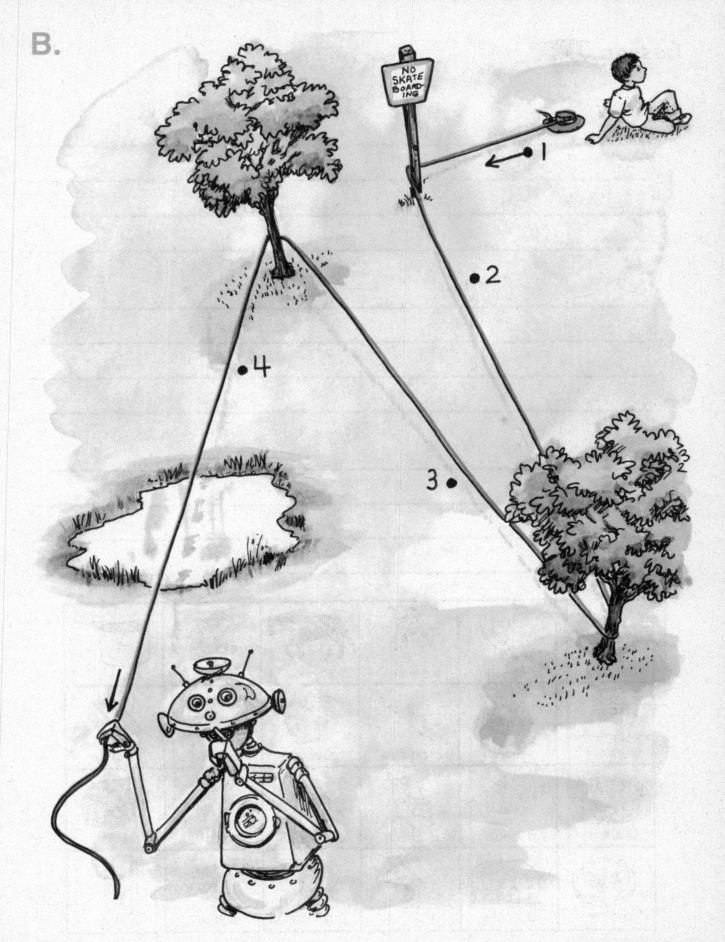

Lesson 21

A.

1.

_____

_____

_____

2.

_____

_____

_____

3.

_____

_____

_____

a hot dog	a chicken	a bike	a horse	a toad	a pot
a note	a mouse	a paddle	an apple	a cow	a ladder
a tub	a book	a chair	an ant	a bottle	a barn
a dime	a house	a puppy	a cup	a plum	a door

B.

Lesson 22

A.

Hounds

1. Greyhound
2. Beagle
3. Basset

Work dogs

1. Collie
2. German shepherd
3. Saint Bernard

B.

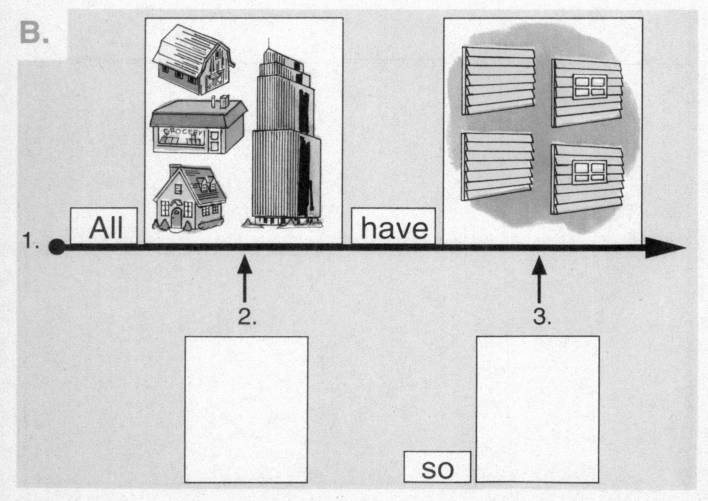

1. | All | | have | |
2.
3.

SO

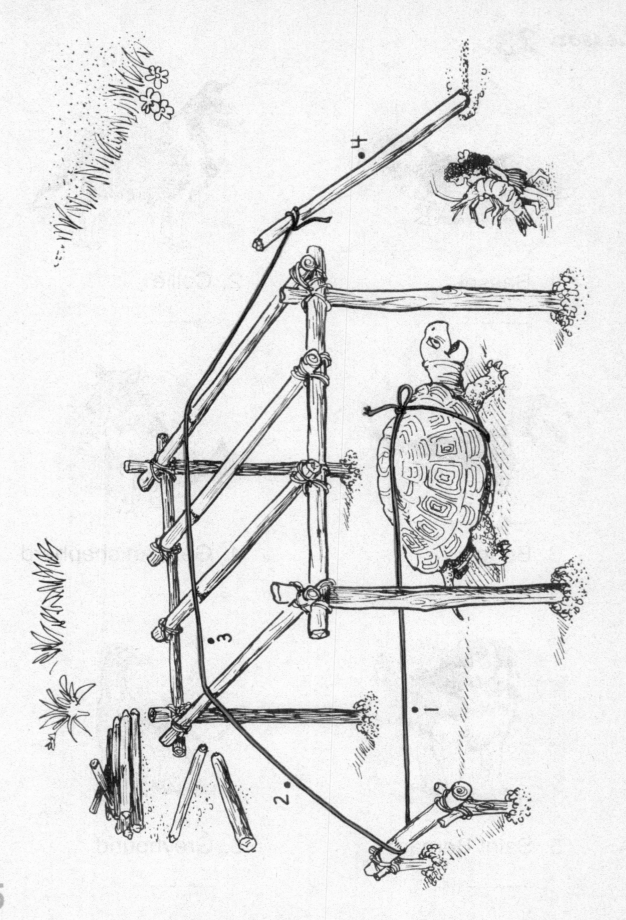

C.

Lesson 23

A.

1. Basset

_____

2. Collie

_____

3. Beagle

_____

4. German shepherd

_____

5. Saint Bernard

_____

6. Greyhound

_____

B.

toadstool 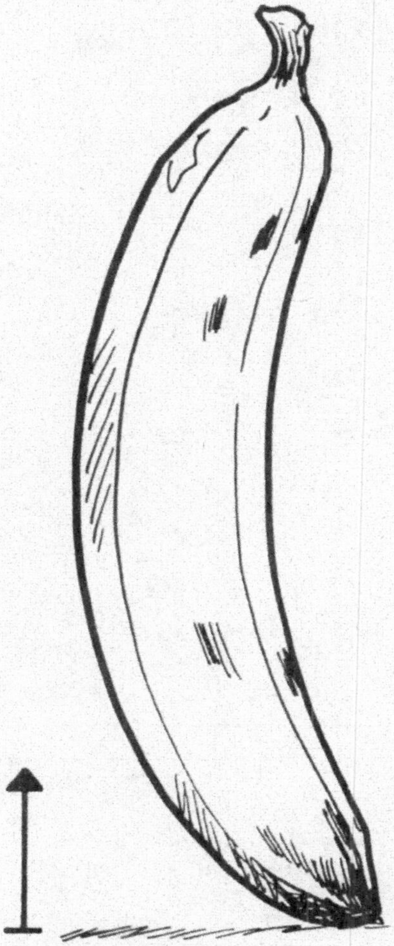   banana 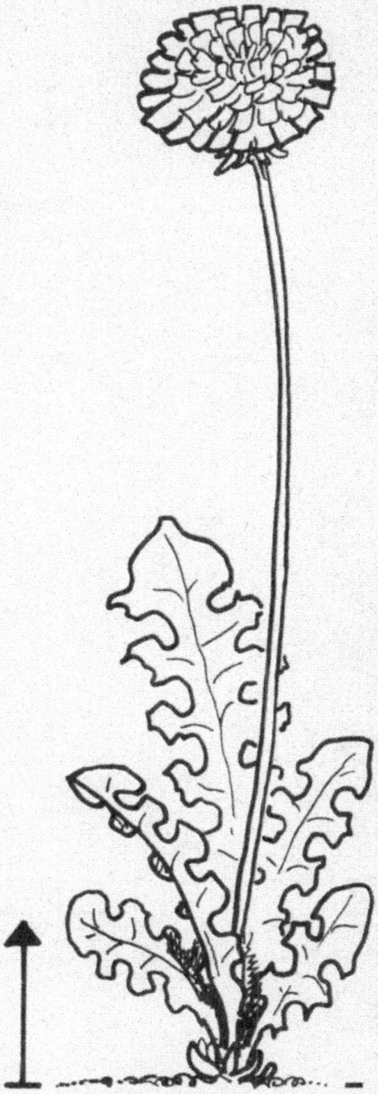   dandelion

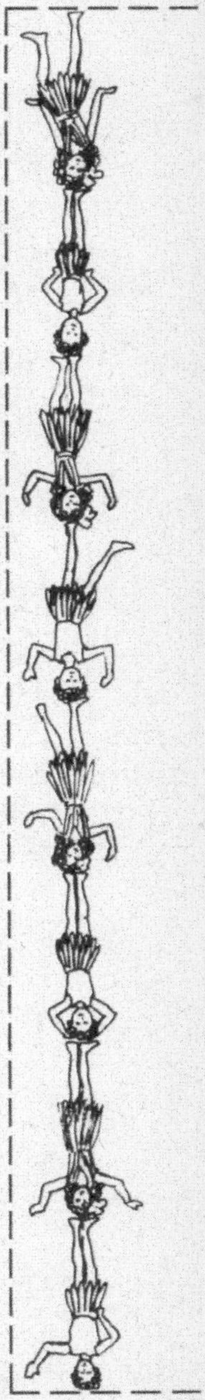

_____,

_____

_____

_____

_____

_____

_____

_____

A.

Class	Not-Class

B.

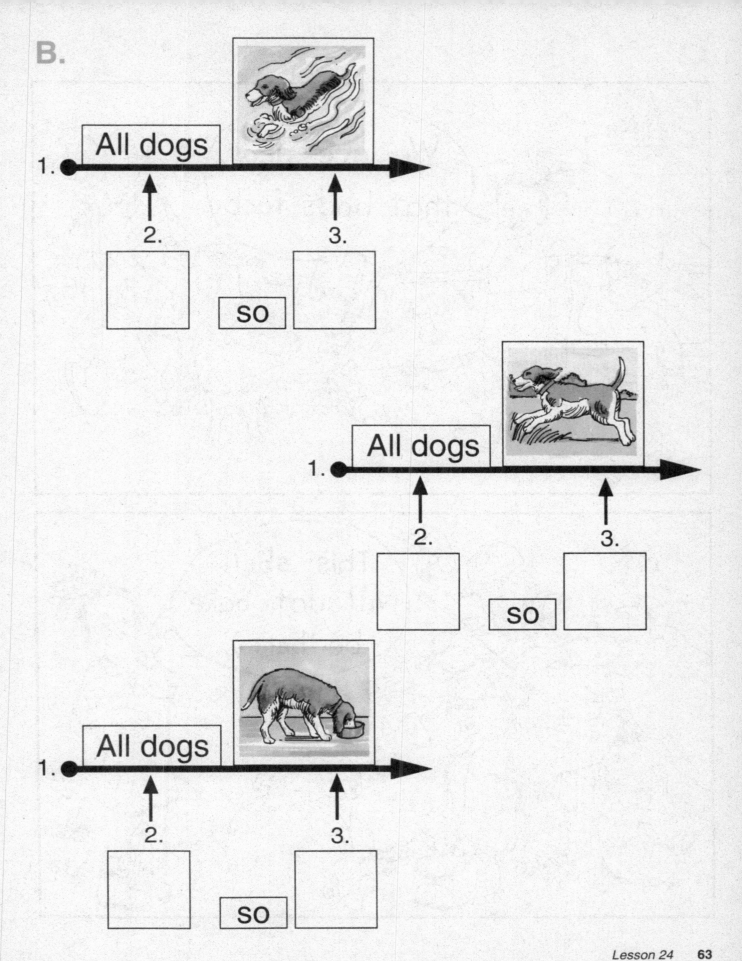

1. All dogs

2.

3.

SO

1. All dogs

2.

3.

SO

1. All dogs

2.

3.

SO

C.

Lesson 25

A.

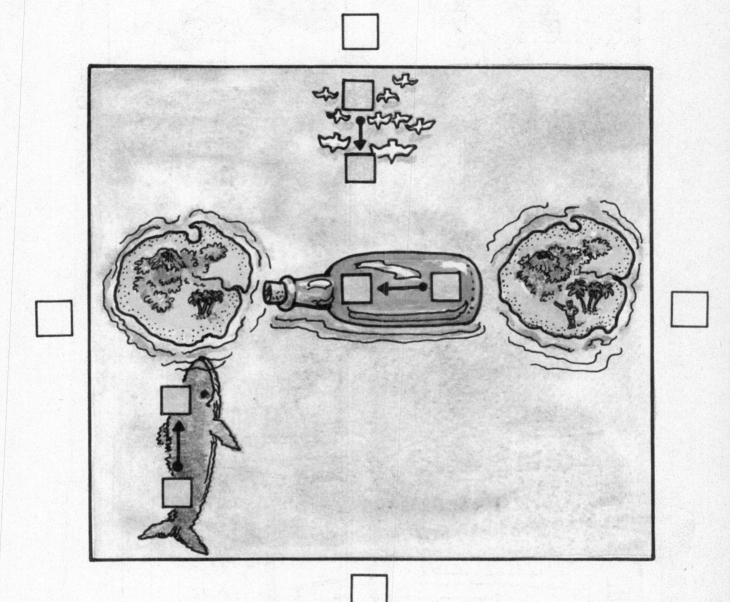

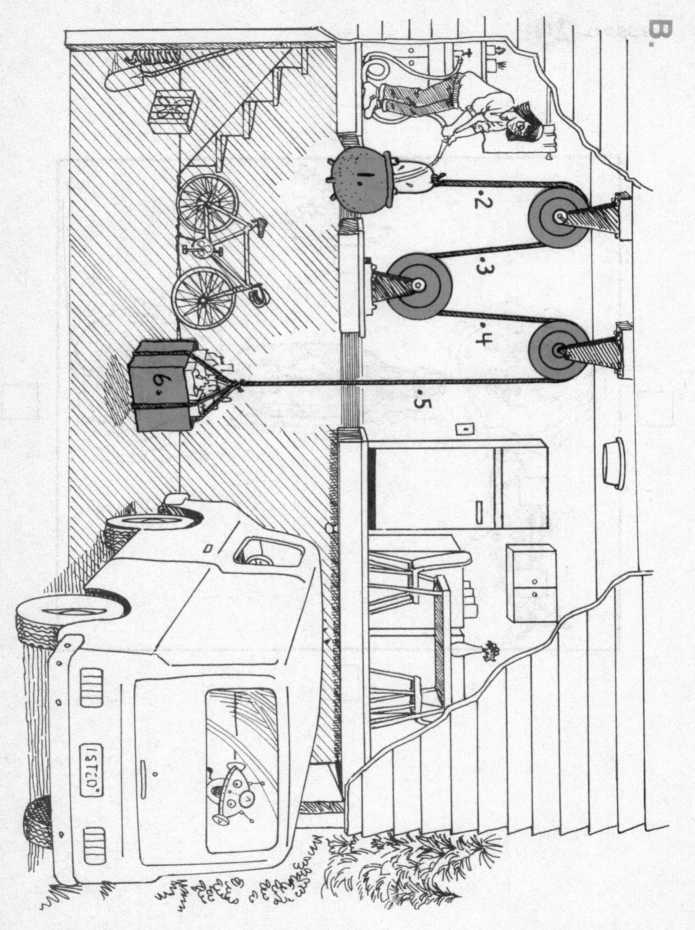

C.

berry bush

 Where is Rod the red bug in the afternoon?

- In the afternoon, all the red bugs are _____

- Rod is _____

- So in the afternoon, Rod is _____

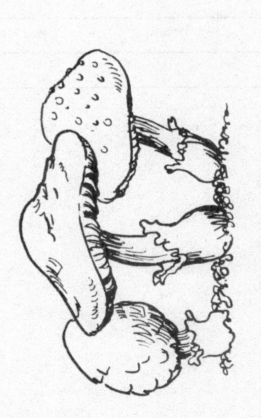

toadstools

 Where is Jenny the toad in the afternoon?

- In the afternoon, all the toads are _____

- Jenny is _____

- So in the afternoon, Jenny is _____

Lesson 26

A.

1.

_____

_____

_____

2.

_____

_____

_____

3.

_____

_____

_____

_____

B.

a truck	a horse	Clarabelle	a skunk	in
Roger	water	a tent	a tree	under
a barn	Owen	a tub	a cage	between
an elephant	a pond	a hole	Molly	next to
a birdbath	a basket	a junkyard	a fishbowl	on
Fizz & Liz	a bottle	a mountain	a bike	over
a ski lodge	an island	a boat	a train	behind
a toadstool	a toaster	a violin	a cow	to
a store	a garage	an airplane	a lake	up
Paul	a box	a ladder	Goober	down

A.

B.

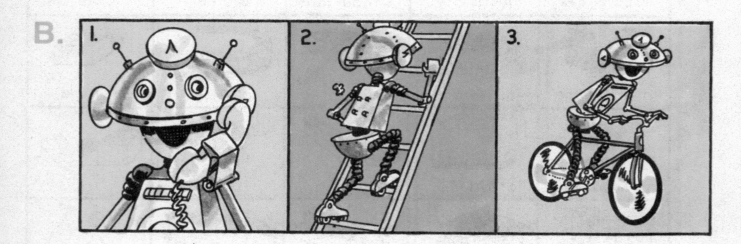

1. Bleep climbed a ladder after he _____
_____.

2. Bleep rode a bike after he _____
_____.

C.

Not-Class

Class

1. _____
2. _____
3. _____

Lesson 28

A.

1. Clarabelle jumped into a pond after she _____ _____.

2. Clarabelle climbed a tree after she _____ _____.

B.

oak tree

lily pads

A. Where is Bonnie the bluebird in the afternoon?

1. In the afternoon, all the bluebirds are in the oak tree.

2. Bonnie is a _____.

3. So in the afternoon, _____.

B. Where is Fran the frog in the afternoon?

1. In the afternoon, all the frogs are _____.

2. Fran is a _____.

3. So in the afternoon, _____.

Lesson 29

A.

toadstools   oak tree

A. Where is Tammy the toad in the morning?

1. In the morning, all the toads are _____.

2. Tammy is a _____.

3. So in the morning, Tammy is _____.

B. Where is Bonnie the bluebird in the morning?

1. In the morning, all the bluebirds are _____.

2. Bonnie is a _____.

3. So in the morning, Bonnie is _____.

B.

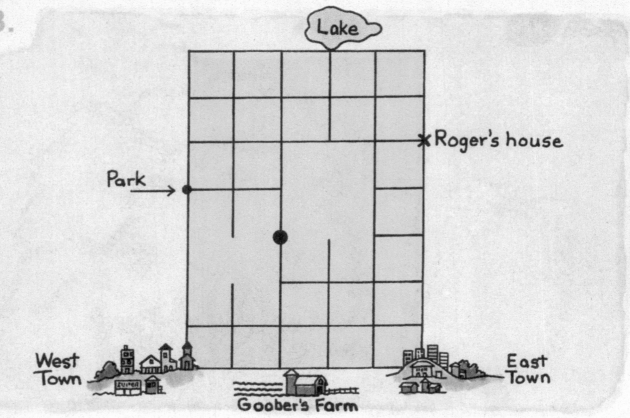

1. To go to Roger's house, you go ___ miles _____.
   Then you go ___ miles _____.

2. To go to West Town, you go ___ miles _____.
   Then you go ___ miles _____.

C.

Collie   Saint Bernard

D.

Test Score

A.

B.

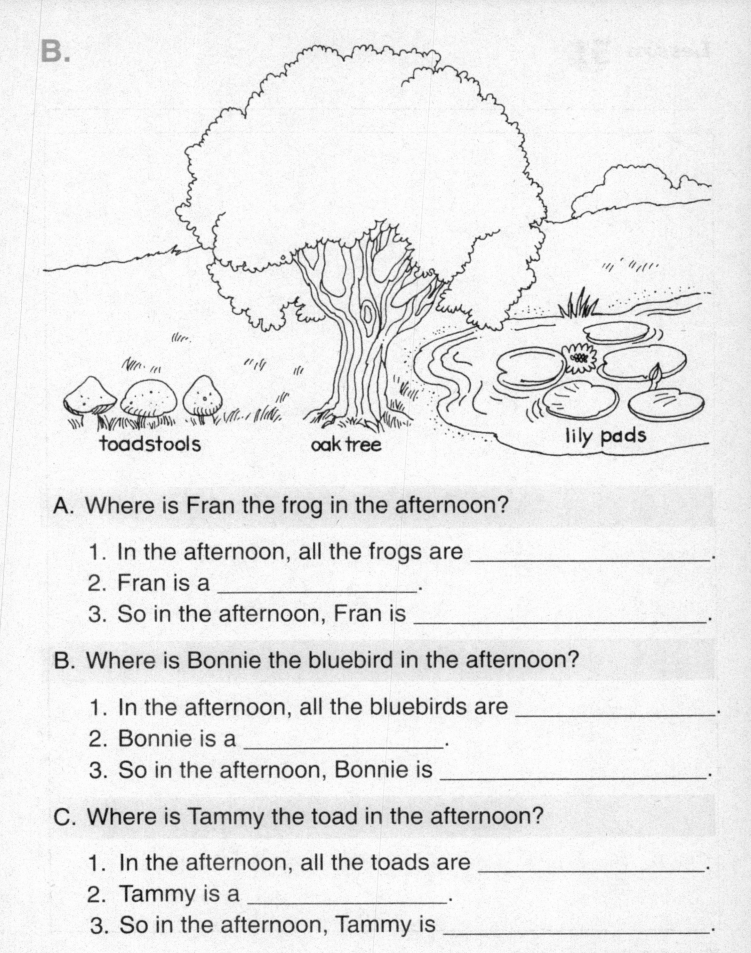

toadstools   oak tree   lily pads

A. Where is Fran the frog in the afternoon?

1. In the afternoon, all the frogs are _____.
2. Fran is a _____.
3. So in the afternoon, Fran is _____.

B. Where is Bonnie the bluebird in the afternoon?

1. In the afternoon, all the bluebirds are _____.
2. Bonnie is a _____.
3. So in the afternoon, Bonnie is _____.

C. Where is Tammy the toad in the afternoon?

1. In the afternoon, all the toads are _____.
2. Tammy is a _____.
3. So in the afternoon, Tammy is _____.

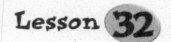

A.

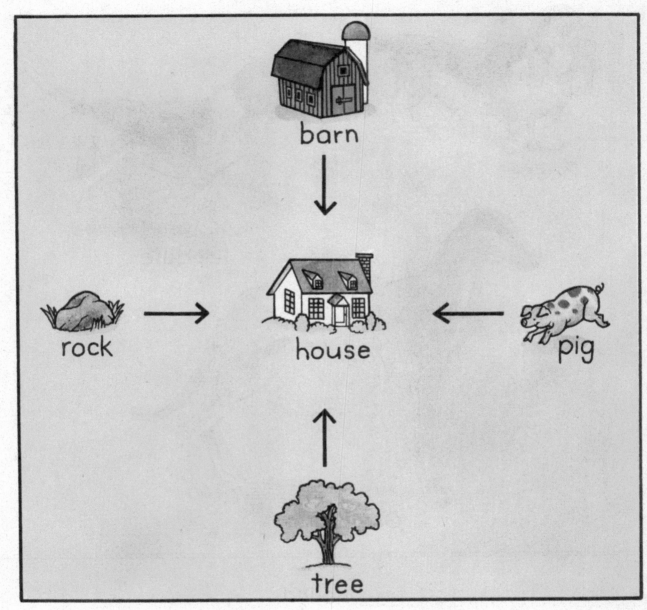

1. The house is west of _____.

2. The house is north of _____.

3. The house is east of _____.

4. The house is south of _____.

B. # Class

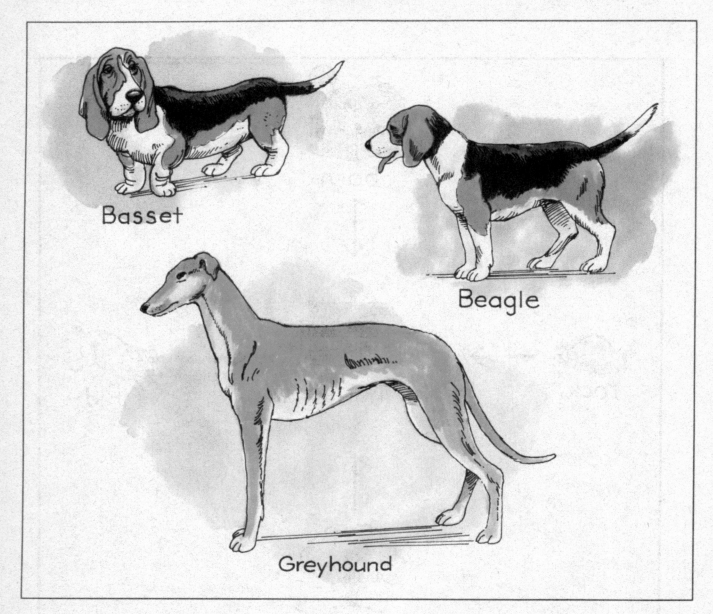

Basset

Beagle

Greyhound

_____ hounds

_____ fast-running hounds

_____ dogs

_____ animals

C.

A.

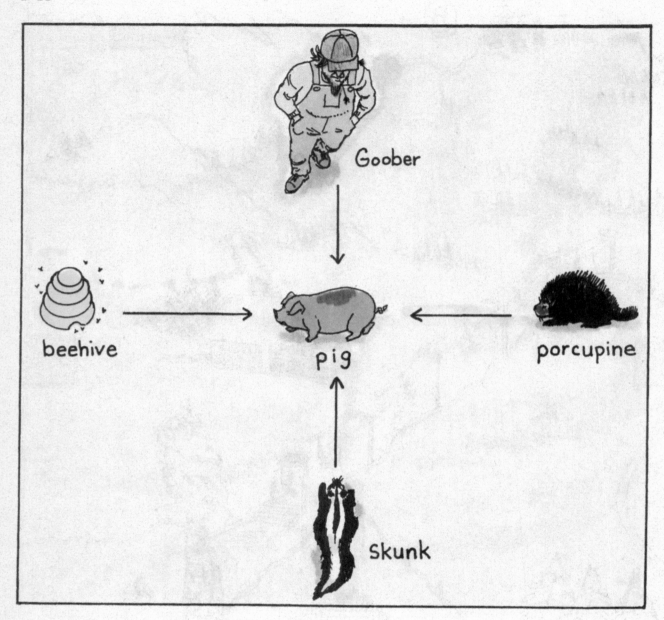

1. The pig is south of _____.

2. The pig is north of _____.

3. The pig is west of _____.

4. The pig is east of _____.

B.

Collie

Saint Bernard

German shepherd

_____ work dogs

_____ animals

_____ work dogs with ears that stand straight up

_____ dogs

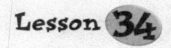

A.

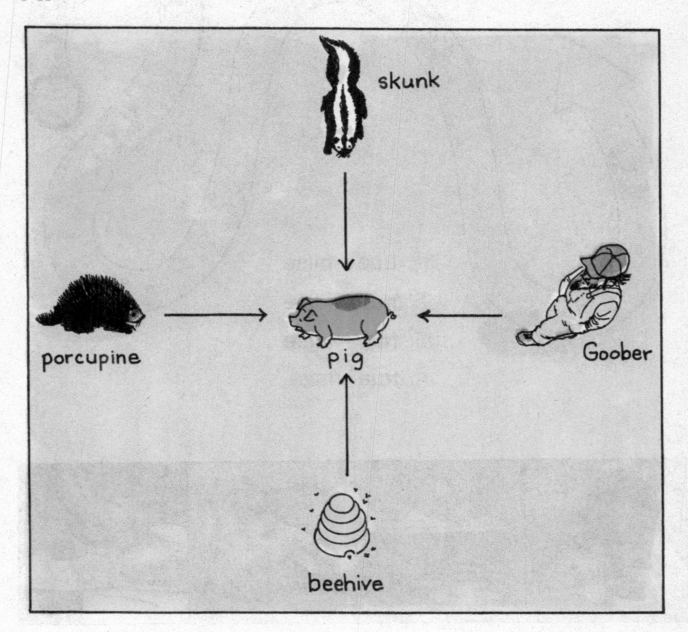

1. The pig is east of _____.

2. The pig is north of _____.

3. The pig is west of _____.

4. The pig is south of _____.

B.

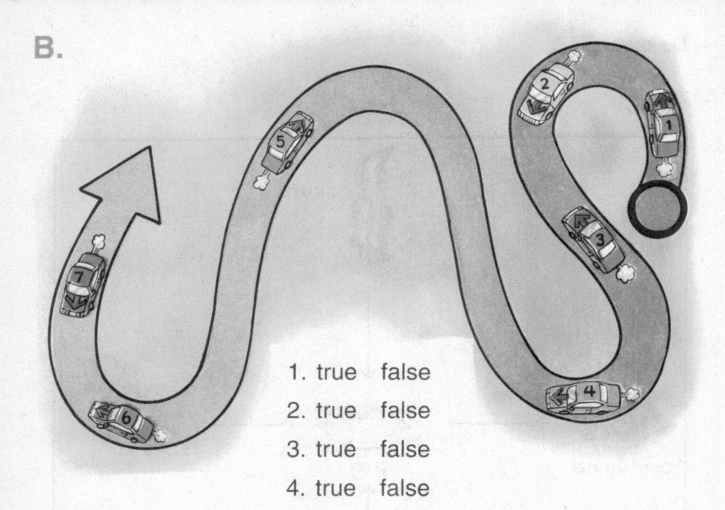

1. true   false
2. true   false
3. true   false
4. true   false

C.

1. Goober _____
   after he milked a cow.
2. Goober _____
   after he played the violin.
3. Goober _____
   after he took a bath.

D.

1. My brother and my sister had pet pigs. <u>They</u> just loved to roll around in the mud.

2. We always kept a glass on top of the refrigerator. We kept <u>it</u> full of water.

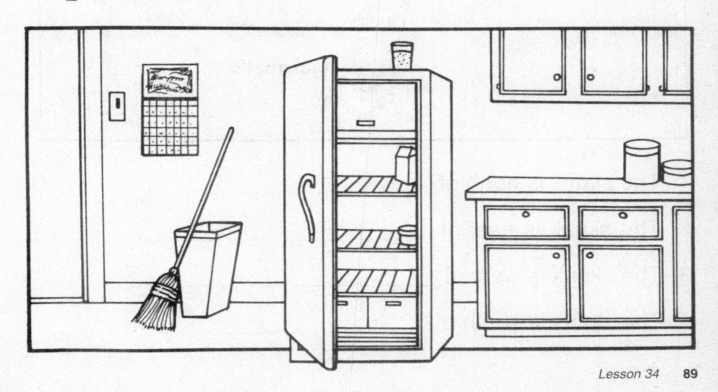

A.

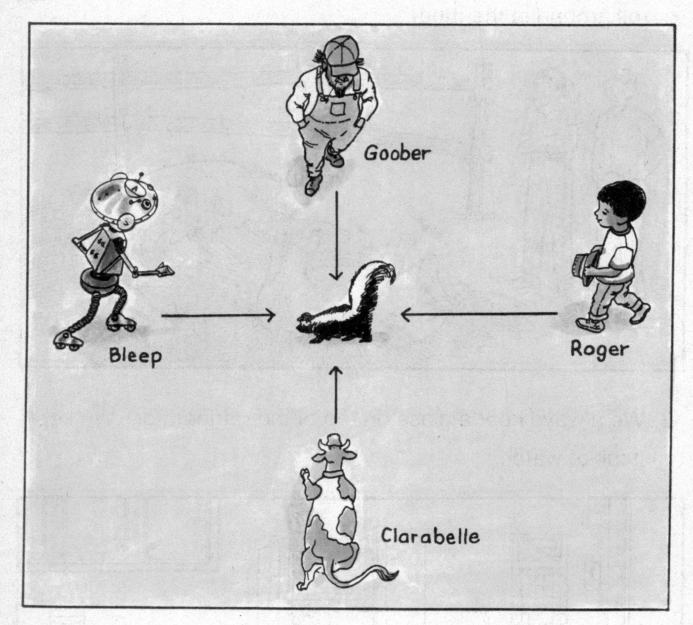

1. The skunk is north of _____.

2. The skunk is east of _____.

3. The skunk is west of _____.

4. The skunk is south of _____.

B.

A.

This thing is in the class of bikes.

_____

B.

This thing is in the class of black bikes.

_____

C.

This thing is in the class of black bikes with a flat front tire.

_____

D.

This thing is in the class of black bikes with a flat front tire and_____

_____

1.

2.

3.

4.

5.

6.

7.

8.

C.

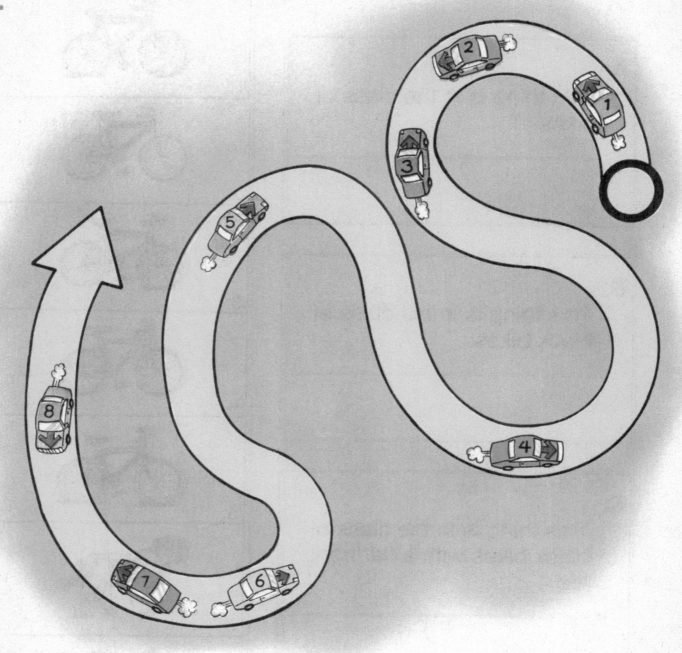

1. true   false

2. true   false

3. true   false

4. true   false

D.

1. My brother and my sister had pet pigs. <u>They</u> just loved to roll around in the mud.

2. We always kept a glass on top of the refrigerator. We kept <u>it</u> full of water.

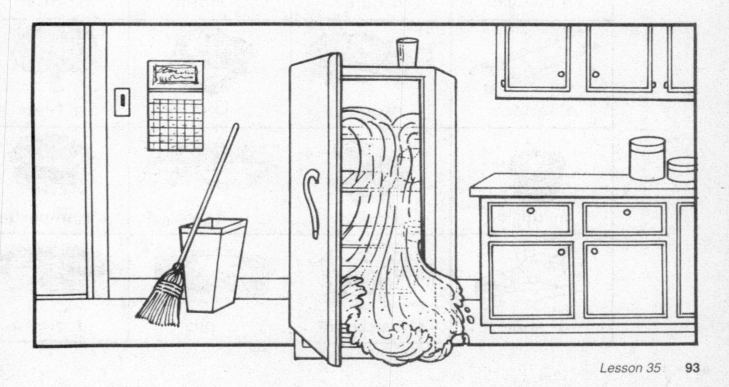

Story words

a rock	a fish	a hat	a farm
a dress	a bottle	a goat	Mrs. Hudson
a coat	Zelda	a house	a plum
Dot	a bone	a stick	a hot dog
a picture	a note	a violin	Goober
a ladder	money	Dud	a tree
an apple	a toad	a town	a hamburger
a shoe	an elephant	a pie	a pizza